THE UNIVERSE *ROCKS!*

SPACECRAFT AND THE JOURNEY INTO SPACE

RAMAN PRINJA

QEB Publishing

To Kamini, Vikas and Sachin

Editorial and Design: Windmill Books Ltd.
Illustrator (activities): Geraint Ford/The Art Agency

First published in the United States in 2012 by
QEB Publishing, Inc.
3 Wrigley, Suite A
Irvine, CA 92618

www.qed-publishing.co.uk

A CIP record for this book is available from the Library of Congress.

ISBN 978 1 60992 246 7

Printed in China

Picture credits (t=top, b=bottom, l=left, c=center, fc=front cover)
Corbis: Li Gang/Xinhua Press 25t; ESA: Cassini Huygens 16t; ESO: Iztok Boncina 6-7;
MPIfR: Jodrell Bank Centre for Astrophysics, University of Manchester 21t; NASA: 4-5,
Apollo Gallery 18bl, GRIN 12b, 24-25, 25br, 30-31, 32; HSF/ISS Imagery: 2-3, 12-13, 13tr, 25cl,
26-27t, Hubble Site: 1, 5tr, 10-11, JPL 16-17, NIX 10bl, 11tr, 15t, 28-29, Pat Rawlings/Image of
the Day Gallery Exploration Imagery 18-19, Science News 22-23; W.M. Keck Observatory/
Rick Peerson: 7tr; Science Photolibrary: RIA Novosti 24bl, Detlev Van Ravensway 23;
Shutterstock: Paulo Afonso 5br, Vinicius Tupinamba 9.
We have made every attempt to contact the copyright holder. If anyone has any
information please contact smortimer@windmillbooks.co.uk

Website information is correct at time of going to press. However, the publishers
cannot accept liability for any information or links found on any Internet sites,
including third-party websites.

In preparation of this book, all due care has been exercised with regard to the
activities and advice depicted. The publishers regret that they can accept no
liability for any loss or injury sustained.

Words in **bold**
are explained in
the glossary on
page 31

What is a Light-year?

Distances in space are measured in light-years.
A light-year is the distance that light travels in one year.

- In one second light travels 186,000 miles
  (300,000 kilometers) or seven times around Earth.
- In one minute light travels 11 million miles (18 million
  kilometers) or to the Moon and back 50 times.
- In one year light travels 5,600 billion miles (9,000
  billion kilometers) or one light-year.

CONTENTS

LET THERE BE LIGHT

We live in very exciting times for exploring space and making amazing discoveries about the Universe.

Scientists use remarkably powerful **telescopes** to study distant **galaxies** and stars. We also launch **spacecraft** from Earth to **orbit** and even land on the planets and moons in our Solar System. In this book we will learn about some of the biggest telescopes used to study the Universe and fly along with spacecraft missions that explore the Solar System. We also look at some new ways scientists are making exciting discoveries in space.

Fuel tank

Space shuttle

Launch tower

Hot gases from engines push the spacecraft upward.

Can't We Just Go There?

The stars and galaxies are unimaginably vast distances away from us. Even light, which travels at 186,000 miles (300,000 kilometers) a second, takes millions of years to reach us from some objects in the huge Universe. Our spacecraft are far too slow to visit these places. However, spacecraft can be flown to planets and moons in our Solar System because they are much closer than the stars.

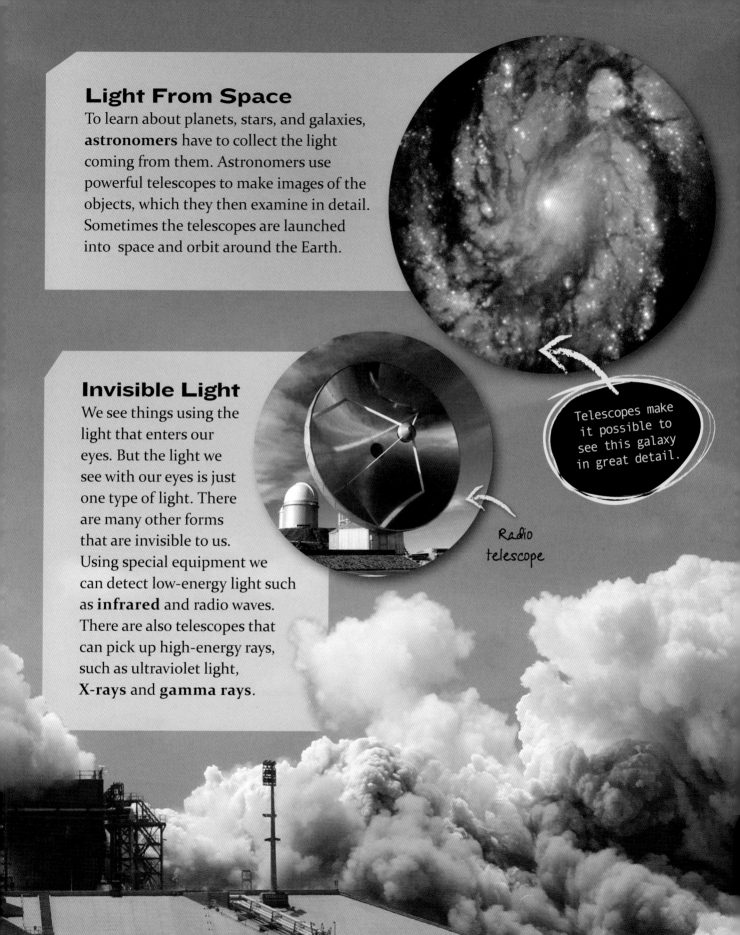

Light From Space

To learn about planets, stars, and galaxies, **astronomers** have to collect the light coming from them. Astronomers use powerful telescopes to make images of the objects, which they then examine in detail. Sometimes the telescopes are launched into space and orbit around the Earth.

Invisible Light

We see things using the light that enters our eyes. But the light we see with our eyes is just one type of light. There are many other forms that are invisible to us. Using special equipment we can detect low-energy light such as **infrared** and radio waves. There are also telescopes that can pick up high-energy rays, such as ultraviolet light, **X-rays** and **gamma rays**.

Telescopes make it possible to see this galaxy in great detail.

Radio telescope

LIGHT BUCKETS

Since the telescope was invented more than 400 years ago, larger and larger machines have been built to study the Universe.

You can think of a telescope as a large bucket that collects light! Telescopes are instruments used by astronomers to make distant objects appear bigger and faraway things seem closer. Telescopes allow us to see incredible things in space that cannot be seen with human eyes alone.

This observatory in Chile is nearly 2 miles (3000 meters) up a mountain where there is a clear view of the sky.

How Do Telescopes Work?

Telescopes use mirrors or **lenses** to see distant objects. Bigger telescopes collect more light from a star, making the image a lot clearer. Most telescopes have two main pieces. They have a large mirror that collects light and reflects it into a sharp point called a focus. The second part is an eyepiece that makes the focused light appear larger.

Keck observatory, Hawaii

Great Observatories

Today's astronomers use giant telescopes that have mirrors 33 feet (10 meters) wide. The telescopes are kept inside huge domes called observatories. Many observatories are perched on high mountains, well away from the glare of lights in cities. These observatories also use other scientific equipment and powerful computers to make the telescopes work.

How Powerful Are the Telescopes?

The best modern observatories have remarkable power. They can turn very faint objects in space into sharp, detailed pictures. The giant Keck telescopes in Hawaii are so powerful they could see the flame of a normal candle placed as far away as the Moon! The 26 foot (8 meter) wide VLT telescope in Chile allows us to see objects four billion times fainter than those we can see with our eyes alone.

MAKE A RAINBOW

We have learnt that astronomers study many different types of light. Even the visible white light we see with our eyes is made up of many colors.

You Will Need:

* A wide glass bowl
* Water
* White cardstock
* A small hand mirror
* Sticky tack
* Sunshine

TRY DOING THIS...

In this activity you can make your own rainbow to see how the white light in sunshine can be split into red, orange, yellow, green, blue, indigo, and violet.

1. Place the glass bowl on a table in a sunny position.

2. Put the hand mirror in the bowl, making sure it leans at a small angle against the side of the bowl. Keep the mirror in place by using sticky tack on the back of the mirror.

Mirror ---

Tack

3. Fill the glass bowl with water until the whole of the mirror is covered. Turn the bowl to keep the mirror directly in the sunlight.

A rainbow is made by white light splitting when it shines through raindrops.

Invisible Light

If you had a special camera, you could see the invisible light in a rainbow. Just beyond the red side of a rainbow there is infrared (below red) light. Beyond the violet light there are ultraviolet (above violet) rays.

4 Now hold the white cardstock next to the bowl on the opposite side from the mirror. Move the cardstock around until you can see the reflection of sunlight from the mirror on the cardstock.

5 You should see a small image on the cardstock that looks like part of a rainbow!

...WHAT DID YOU LEARN?

The white sunlight reflects off the mirror in the bowl, and as it passes up through the water the light is bent. This makes the white light split up into the colors of the rainbow. Something similar happens when the Sun comes out during rain. The sunlight strikes droplets of rain and is broken up into a set of colors. We see this as a rainbow arching across the sky.

TELESCOPES IN SPACE

Some telescopes are launched into space on board rockets and placed into orbit around the Earth.

Different types of space telescope study different types of light. Telescopes that can see X-rays and ultraviolet light are used to study the hottest stars, such as exploding supernovae. Infrared-sensing telescopes reveal how stars are born out of cool clouds of gas. Earth's **atmosphere** blurs the light shining through it, so putting a telescope in space above the atmosphere means we can see objects much more clearly.

Light comes in here

Chandra X-ray Observatory

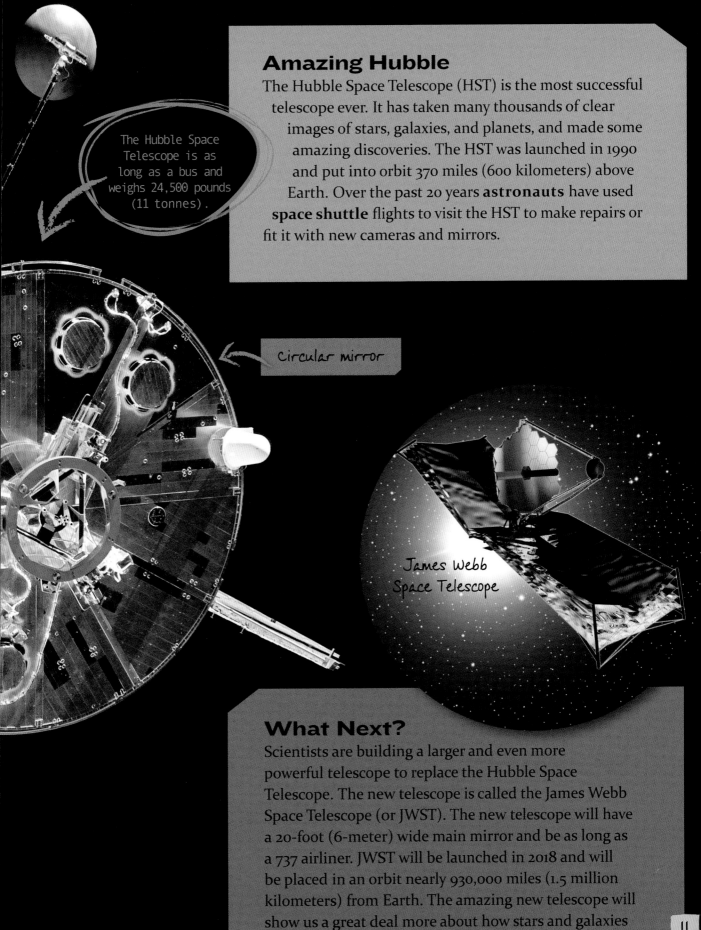

Amazing Hubble

The Hubble Space Telescope (HST) is the most successful telescope ever. It has taken many thousands of clear images of stars, galaxies, and planets, and made some amazing discoveries. The HST was launched in 1990 and put into orbit 370 miles (600 kilometers) above Earth. Over the past 20 years **astronauts** have used **space shuttle** flights to visit the HST to make repairs or fit it with new cameras and mirrors.

The Hubble Space Telescope is as long as a bus and weighs 24,500 pounds (11 tonnes).

Circular mirror

James Webb Space Telescope

What Next?

Scientists are building a larger and even more powerful telescope to replace the Hubble Space Telescope. The new telescope is called the James Webb Space Telescope (or JWST). The new telescope will have a 20-foot (6-meter) wide main mirror and be as long as a 737 airliner. JWST will be launched in 2018 and will be placed in an orbit nearly 930,000 miles (1.5 million kilometers) from Earth. The amazing new telescope will show us a great deal more about how stars and galaxies are made.

Space Stations

Space stations are large spacecraft that allow astronauts to live and work in space for long periods of time.

The International Space Station (ISS) is the largest object ever built in space. It is so big that more than 40 rockets and space shuttle flights were needed to carry all the parts into space. The ISS was built by many countries working together. It is almost the size of a football pitch and can even be seen in the night sky from Earth! There are several different rooms called modules where astronauts live, work and sleep.

cooling panels

Valery Polyakov looks out of the window of *Mir*, the Russian space station where he lived.

Living in Space

There is no gravity inside a space station, so the astronauts float. This means they don't use their muscles much. The astronauts' bodies can become weak after a long time in space, and so the crew does lots of exercise every day. Russian Valery Polyakov spent 438 days living in space—longer than anyone else. He orbited Earth 7075 times and travelled 186 million miles (300 million kilometers)!

Solar panel

The
astronauts strap
their sleeping bags to
the wall to stop them
floating around.

Space laboratory

Supply
module

Crew transporter

Washing and Eating

To save as much water as possible, the ISS crew cannot take showers, but wash with a damp cloth instead. Space food is not too different from what we eat on Earth. There are more than 100 items on the space station's food menu, including frozen vegetables and yogurts.

13

BALLOON ROCKET

Rockets blasting off from Earth are an amazing sight. They can weigh hundreds of tons at liftoff, but hot gases pushed out at very high speeds have enough power to lift the rocket off the ground.

TRY DOING THIS...

Rockets normally burn a fuel made of liquid hydrogen and liquid oxygen. In this activity you can explore how a rocket works using air as the fuel!

You Will Need:

* About 16 feet (5 m) of strong string
* A few plastic straws (not bendy ones)
* Sticky tape
* Some balloons with a mixture of long and rounded shapes

1 Tie one end of the string to a fixture in the room such as a chair or door handle.

3 Cut two pieces of sticky tape. Now blow up the balloon and pinch the end so that the air does not come out. Tape the balloon under the straw using the tape. You might need some help with the tape while you hold the balloon.

2 Thread the other end of the string through the straw and pull it tight. Tie the loose end of the string to another fixed object, keeping it tight. Move the straw to the middle of the string.

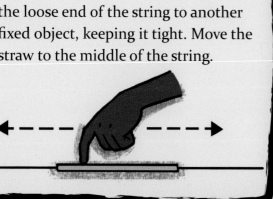

4 You're now ready for launch. Let go of the balloon and watch it fly across the room.

...WHAT DID YOU LEARN?

Like all rockets, your balloon rocket works because of **thrust**. Thrust is the force that moves the rocket. The air pushing out from the balloon gives thrust to move your rocket. The burning fuel in real rockets blasts hot gases down toward the ground. The hot blast pushes the rocket upward.

Further Experiments

Try to experiment with different shapes of balloon, filling the balloon with more or less air, and changing the size of the straw by cutting it in half or quarter. See how the speed and distance traveled by the balloon changes.

MISSIONS TO THE PLANETS

Over the past 50 years we have made fantastic new discoveries about planets by sending spacecraft to explore the Solar System.

Spacecraft have been sent to every planet in the Solar System. We've even landed probes on the surfaces of Venus, Mars, and Saturn's moon Titan, and visited some asteroids and comets. None of these missions carried any astronauts. The Moon is the only place beyond Earth that has been visited by humans. Between July 1969 and December 1972, twelve astronauts walked on the Moon. No one has been back to the Moon since.

Beyond the Solar System

Some spacecraft have actually left the Solar System. The *Voyager 1* probe was launched in 1977 and is now over 100 times farther from the Sun than Earth is. The *Pioneer 11* spacecraft, launched in 1975, is now more than 6.8 billion miles (11 billion km) away from Earth. This probe is carrying drawings of humans. Who knows, maybe one day it will be found by an alien civilisation!

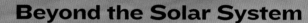

The Huygens lander parachuted to the surface of Titan—and found lakes full of oil!

Keeping a Close Eye on Mars

More spacecraft missions have been sent to Mars than to any other planet. Using orbiters and **landers**, astronomers have learned a great deal about the atmosphere and surface of Mars, and have even found tiny amounts of water ice. Since 2004 **rovers** have also been driving around on the surface of Mars. Like radio-controlled cars, the rovers get instructions from Earth telling them to move to new locations and examine rocks and soil.

Camera arm

Radio dish

Solar panel

This Mars rover is called *Opportunity*. Its job is to study the surface of Mars.

WHERE TO NEXT?

Scientists are planning to launch even more amazing spacecraft. In the future, faster rockets and clever robots will let us explore more of the Solar System.

A crewed mission to another planet, such as Mars, would be difficult. Spacecraft carrying fuel, water, and building materials would be sent first. Only then could a crew set off. It takes nearly seven months to fly there. There is no oxygen on Mars so the base would need machines to recycle air and water. Vegetables could be grown in greenhouses. The crew would live underground to stay safe from dangerous radiation.

Training on the Moon

Back to the Moon

Many scientists think that returning to the Moon is an important way to train for a Mars mission. The Moon and Mars are similar. Both have **gravity** that is weaker than that on Earth. There is no air to breathe on the Moon, so it's a good place to learn how to survive by purifying water for drinking and turning into rocket fuel. It is also easier to test technologies on the Moon since it is just a three-day rocket ride away.

Drilling on Icy Moons

Scientists plan to drop landers on icy moons of Jupiter and Saturn. They want to drill through their surfaces to reach huge oceans of water that are thought to lie beneath. They may find simple life-forms that survive in the deep, dark alien oceans.

It can get very cold on Mars and the atmosphere is very thin. Without a spacesuit, the astronaut's blood would freeze.

SUPER HEARING

Spacecraft send back very weak radio signals to Earth, and it can be difficult to pick up the tiny whispers from the distant spacecraft.

You Will Need:

* A large 16 x 24 inches (41 x 61 cm) piece of thin cardstock
* Sticky tape
* A friend to help make sounds

1 Roll the cardstock into the shape of a cone. Leave a 0.8 inch (2 cm) hole at the pointed end and make the large end of the cone as wide as possible.

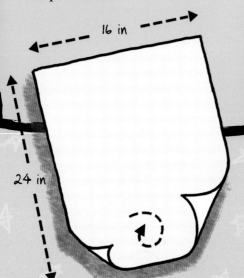

16 in

24 in

2 Use the sticky tape to secure the edge of the cardstock so that the cone does not open up.

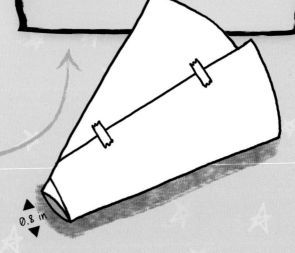

0.8 in

Dish Detectors

Spacecraft travel millions or even billions of miles from Earth. Very large dish-shaped receivers called **antennae** are pointed at the sky to detect the weak signals.

> The dish collects weak radio signals and directs them to a detection antenna in the center.

3 Go outside and listen to some sounds, first with just your ears and then by placing the cone against your ear. Get a friend to stand many feet away and make very weak sounds, like gently tapping a couple of pebbles together.

Ask a friend to help.

click click

4 Notice how much easier it is to hear the tapping sound with your cone. See how far away your friend can walk while you can still hear the sound. Now try to listen without the cone.

...WHAT DID YOU LEARN?

The shape of the cone helps to move the sound waves to a point near your ear. Because the radio signals from spacecraft are so weak, the antennae have to be very large, like using a huge cone! The largest antennae are 230 feet (70 meters) across.

SAILING TO THE STARS

Today's spacecraft take several years to reach the planets. To travel to stars we will need new, much faster spaceships.

The stars are very far away. The nearest star to the Sun, called Proxima Centauri, is almost 100,000 times farther away than the outer planet Neptune. Using current rocket engines it would take more than 20,000 years to reach Proxima Centauri!

Solar Sails

A new way of getting spacecraft to move much faster in space is to use solar sails. A solar sail is made of a huge mirror-like surface that is pushed along by light. The force is produced by sunlight reflecting off the shiny side of the sail. Gradually, as more and more sunlight hits the sail, the spacecraft rises to super-high speeds.

In the future starships might be powered by enormous solar sails built in space.

A space colony, like this artist's impression, would be home to people colonizing a planet.

Laser Powered

A laser can be focused into a very tiny beam of light packed with energy. One day we might be able to launch small but fast spacecraft that are pushed along by lasers shining onto solar sails.

Colonies on the Move

Even a large laser-powered solar sail doing 620,000 miles (1,000 km) per second would take 1,300 years to reach the nearest star. If humans are to travel between stars we will have to build space colonies with farmers, doctors, and teachers on board. None of the people leaving Earth will reach the final destination, but their descendants will.

So You Want to Be an Astronaut?

You don't need superhero powers to become an astronaut. But you will need to work very hard if your dream is to fly into space.

The journey to becoming an astronaut starts very early. You have to study hard at school and do well in subjects like math and science. If you want to be a commander of a spacecraft then you'll have to train to become a top pilot who can fly fast jet aircraft.

Spacewalk training

Cargo bay

Spacewalking

Astronauts learn to spacewalk—or move around outside the spacecraft. They train for this in huge swimming pools, where they float in the same way as in space.

Specialist at work

Astronaut Jobs

The commander is the pilot of the spacecraft and leads the whole mission. There are also mission specialists who carry out experiments in space or go on spacewalks to mend the spacecraft.

Crowded Crew

Living Together

Astronauts have to live and work in very small modules on spacecraft. You will need to enjoy working in a team and be prepared to help others. One thing is for sure—the view from your office in space will be fantastic!

SLEEP AND GROW

We have learned that in space astronauts have to live and work in zero gravity. The force of gravity can affect your height, as this activity will demonstrate.

TRY DOING THIS...

In this activity you can explore how the pull of gravity can change your height in just one day!

You Will Need:

* A flat hard floor and wall to stand against
* Help of an adult
* A hardbacked book
* A pencil
* A measuring tape

1 Find a place in your home with a hard level floor and wall that you can stand against to have your height measured.

2 Last thing at night, just before going to bed, stand upright against the wall and ask an adult to place the book on your head. Keep the book still and move away from the wall.

Ask an adult to help.

Ask an adult to help.

3 Ask the adult to carefully mark the position of the bottom of the book using the pencil. Use the measuring tape to measure the distance from the floor to the pencil mark. This should be an accurate measure of your height at bedtime.

Growing strong

On Earth, gravity helps our bodies to make thick bones and strong muscles. In space without gravity the muscles and bones of the astronauts can become much weaker.

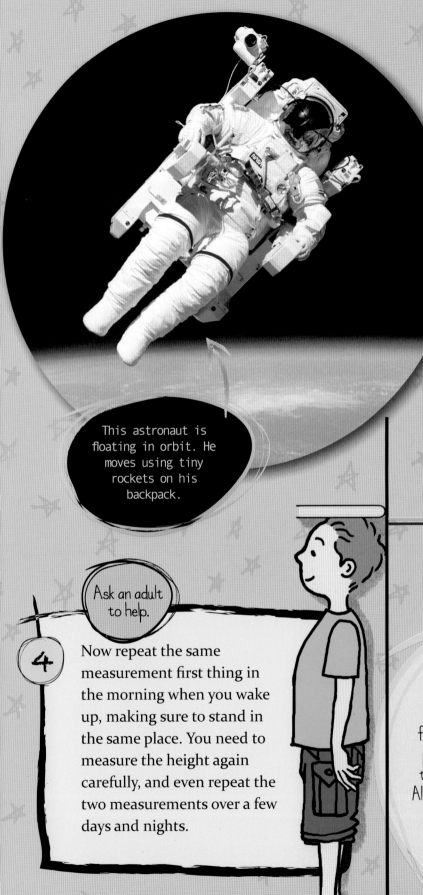

Weightless

When in orbit, astronauts have no weight—gravity does not pull them down, so they just float. It takes a bit of practice to get used to being weightless. Even astronauts experience motion sickness when they first arrive in orbit.

This astronaut is floating in orbit. He moves using tiny rockets on his backpack.

5 Notice how you are about a third of an inch (1 cm) taller when you wake up in the morning than you are last thing at night!

Ask an adult to help.

4 Now repeat the same measurement first thing in the morning when you wake up, making sure to stand in the same place. You need to measure the height again carefully, and even repeat the two measurements over a few days and nights.

WHAT DID YOU LEARN...

You are slightly taller in the morning than at night because of the force of gravity. During the day gravity pulls down on your spine. The bones in the spine are squeezed closer together. All this pushing can make you lose a little height during the day. At night, when you are lying flat, the bones spread out again so you stretch back to full height.

REALLY COOL STUFF ABOUT SPACECRAFT

Spacecraft are amazing machines. Let's take a look at some more facts about these high-tech craft.

Can You See the Pyramids from Space?

The International Space Station orbits about 220 miles (350 km) above Earth, and astronauts on board have used digital cameras to take pictures of the large pyramids in Giza, Egypt. But the farther away in space you go, the less you see on Earth. No human-made object on Earth can be seen from the Moon.

Why Are Spacesuits White?

Astronauts wear white spacesuits because white reflects heat and keeps the astronauts from getting too hot. White spacesuits are also easy to see against the black background of space, which means spacewalkers do not go missing!

How Much Space Junk is There Around the Earth?

There are lots of human-made bits orbiting Earth. This swarm of junk includes old satellites, pieces of rockets, and even a screwdriver that slipped from the hand of an astronaut! There are nearly 500,000 pieces of space junk.

Why Did a Spacecraft Crash into Jupiter?

In 2003, after many years studying the planet, a space probe called Galileo crashed into Jupiter. The probe had run out of fuel. It was crushed by the thick layers of gas around the giant planet.

How Can Gravity Speed up a Spacecraft?

Scientists use the gravity of the Sun and planets to make spacecraft move faster, like a catapult. The spacecraft are flown several times around a planet and then flung out toward its final path.

How Long Would a 747 Jumbo Jet Take to Fly to the Moon?

Planes can't fly to the Moon because there is no air in space to burn their fuel. If you did travel at the speed of a 747 jumbo jet, it would take nearly 18 days to get to the Moon!

Has an Alien Spaceship Ever Landed on the Earth?

Despite what we see in movies, no aliens have ever come to Earth. People see Unidentified Flying Objects (or UFOs), but most turn out to be normal things such as planes, clouds, or the planet Venus!

Will There Be a Mission to the Sun?

No spacecraft has ever been closer to the Sun than the orbit of Mercury. But a new mission called Solar Probe is planned for launch in 2018 and will fly just 5.6 million miles (9 million km) above the surface of the Sun.

How Hot Does a Rocket Engine Get?

It is very difficult to measure the temperature in the middle of a rocket engine that's in full blast. The main engines of the space shuttle burn at an amazing 5970 degrees Fahrenheit (3,300 degrees Celsius) and use up nearly 2.2 million tons (2 million tonnes) of fuel in less than 9 minutes!

Are the Footprints of Astronauts Still on the Moon?

The footprints of the astronauts who went to the Moon will be there for millions of years because there is no wind on the Moon to blow them away.

TOP TEN SPACECRAFT FACTS

1. The tallest rocket ever was *Saturn 5*, which took astronauts to the Moon. *Saturn 5* was 360 feet (110 meters) tall, which is higher than a 30-storey building!

2. The fastest spacecraft is the *New Horizons* mission to Pluto. It moves at nearly 38,000 miles (60,000 kilometers) per hour.

3. The longest spacewalk lasted 8 hours and 56 minutes outside the International Space Station.

4. The most reused spacecraft is the space shuttle *Discovery*, which flew 38 times.

5. The *Mars Odyssey* spacecraft is the longest-working orbiter. It first started orbiting Mars in October 2001.

6. The farthest place a spacecraft has ever touched down is Saturn's giant moon Titan, visited by the *Huygens* lander.

7. The coldest working spacecraft is *Planck*, the scientific instruments of which are kept just above -459 degrees Fahrenheit (–273 degrees Celsius)!

8. At 10.9 billion miles (17.5 billion kilometers), *Voyager 1* is the most distant spacecraft from Earth.

9. The largest space crew ever was when 8 astronauts were launched on the *Challenger* space shuttle.

10. The *Galileo* spacecraft made the fastest entry into an atmosphere. It entered Jupiter's gas layers at nearly 106,000 miles (170,000 kilometers) per hour!

WEBSITES

Hubble Space Telescope Gallery http://hubblesite.org/gallery

European Space Agency http://www.esa.int

BBC Space http://www.bbc.co.uk/science/space/

NASA http://www.nasa.gov/audience/forkids/kidsclub/flash/index.html

National Geographic Space http://science.nationalgeographic.com/science/space/

Online Star Map http://www.open2.net/science/finalfrontier/planisphere/planisphere_embedded.html

GLOSSARY

antenna A large dish that can send or receive radio signals.

astronaut A person who travels in space.

astronomer A scientist who studies objects in space, such as planets and stars.

atmosphere Gases that surround a planet, moon, or star.

galaxy A collection of billions of stars, gas, and dust held together by gravity.

gamma rays High-energy rays that are made by the hottest objects in the Universe.

gravity A force that attracts two objects and that depends on the amount of matter in the objects and how far they are apart.

infrared Light of low energy that is invisible but can be felt as heat.

lander A space vehicle that is designed to land on the surface of a moon or planet.

lens A curved piece of glass that can be used to bend rays of light.

Mir A space station built by Russia and launched in 1986. It was the first space station to be permanently occupied by cosmonauts. Some cosmonauts spent over a year on Mir.

orbit The path taken by an object as it moves around another body. The Moon follows an orbit around the Earth.

rover A space vehicle used to explore the surface of a moon or planet. A rover can have a crew or it can be controlled from Earth.

spacecraft A vehicle for travel beyond the Earth's atmosphere.

space shuttle A space vehicle that took off like a rocket and landed like an aeroplane and carried people into space. There were 135 space shuttle missions between 1981 and 2011, when the shuttle program ended.

telescope A device using lenses and mirrors for viewing objects that are far away.

thrust Force that pushes down when a rocket burns its engines.

X-rays A type of high-energy light that can pass through most solid objects.

INDEX